THE WORLD OF...

History
Revision

Lynn Huggins-Cooper

Good day. I'm Sir Ralph Witherbottom. I'm an accomplished inventor, a dashing discoverer and an enthusiastic entrepreneur.

Hi! I'm Isabella Witherbottom – my friends call me Izzy. I'm Sir Ralph's daughter and I like to keep him on his toes!

And they both keep me on my toes! How do you do? I'm Max, the butler, at your service.

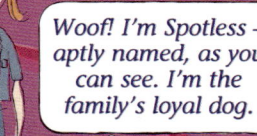

Woof! I'm Spotless – aptly named, as you can see. I'm the family's loyal dog.

Contents

Victorious Victorians 4
Who were the Victorians?

The Good Old Days? 6
Life as a poor Victorian child

School Rules! 8
Victorian schools

Revise Time 10
Revision exercises

Child's Play 12
Victorian toys

Call Yourself a Man? 14
Victorian children's clothes

Amazing Ancestry! 16
The Census

Revise Time 18
Revision exercises

What a Mess! 20
Victorian diseases and hygiene

Left-Over Legacies 22
Things the Victorians left behind

A Grave Situation 24
Local history

Revise Time 26
Revision exercises

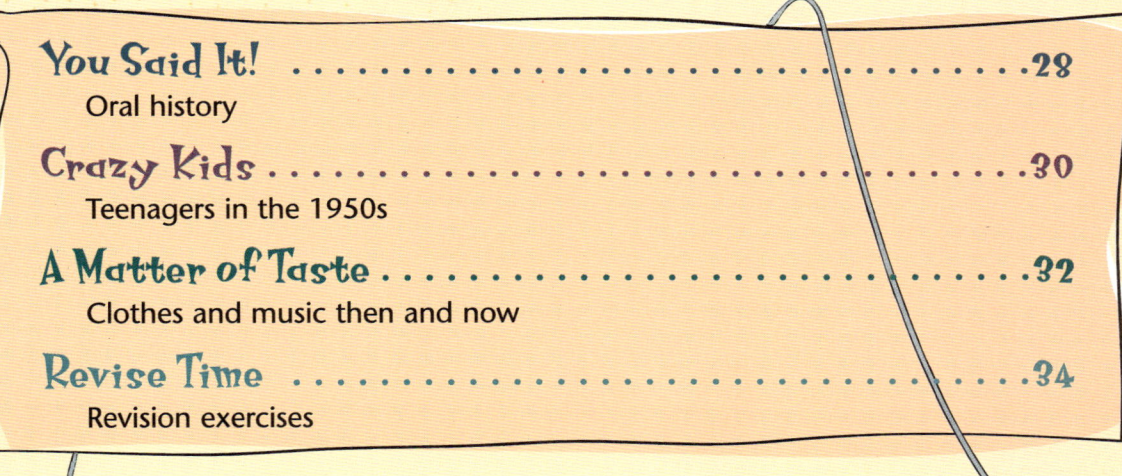

You Said It! 28
Oral history

Crazy Kids 30
Teenagers in the 1950s

A Matter of Taste 32
Clothes and music then and now

Revise Time 34
Revision exercises

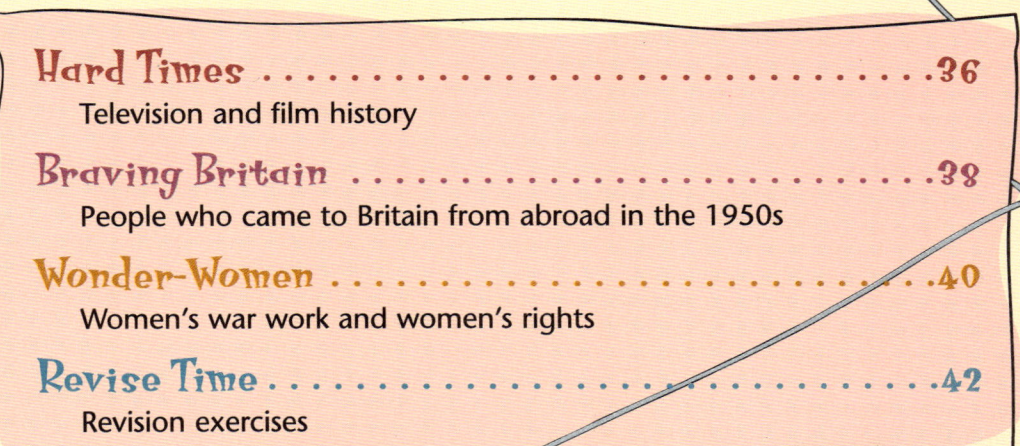

Hard Times 36
Television and film history

Braving Britain 38
People who came to Britain from abroad in the 1950s

Wonder-Women 40
Women's war work and women's rights

Revise Time 42
Revision exercises

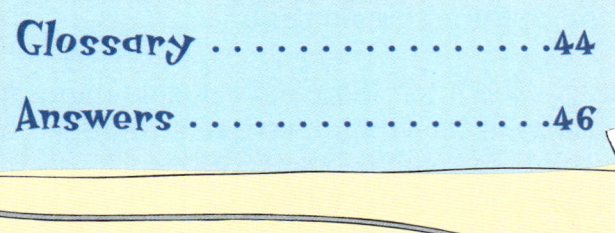

Glossary 44

Answers 46

Victorious Victorians

Isabella is doing a project at school about the Victorians.

"Dad, my teacher set me a question for homework: 'Who were the Victorians?' So far, all I've got is 'people who lived during the **reign** of Queen Victoria'. I don't suppose that's enough…"

"Nor do I! Look here, Izzy," said Sir Ralph Witherbottom, pulling down a large book from the shelf. On the first page, there was a big photograph of Queen Victoria. "Queen Victoria was a great ruler. During her reign, Britain's **empire** grew until it covered one fifth of the world and ruled over more than 370 million people. Look at this map. All the pink parts were part of the British Empire!"

Cocoa beans? For making chocolate? Now that's what I call a valuable cargo!

Isabella looked at the map of the British Empire.

"Wow, dad – the Empire was huge! It contained countries from all over the world, including Canada, Australia, New Zealand, South Africa and India. It's amazing to think that Queen Victoria was the Queen of all of the countries Britain controlled."

"Yes, Izzy – and interesting and valuable things from all the countries in the Empire were sent to Britain on great trading ships. Tea, cocoa beans, cloth such as silk and linen, rubber for factories and precious metals; they were all shipped here. Many **raw materials** were brought here to be made into things that were then sold around the world. Cotton was brought here to be woven into fabric in the great factories."

Colour it in

Using a pink crayon, colour in the countries on the map that were part of the British Empire.

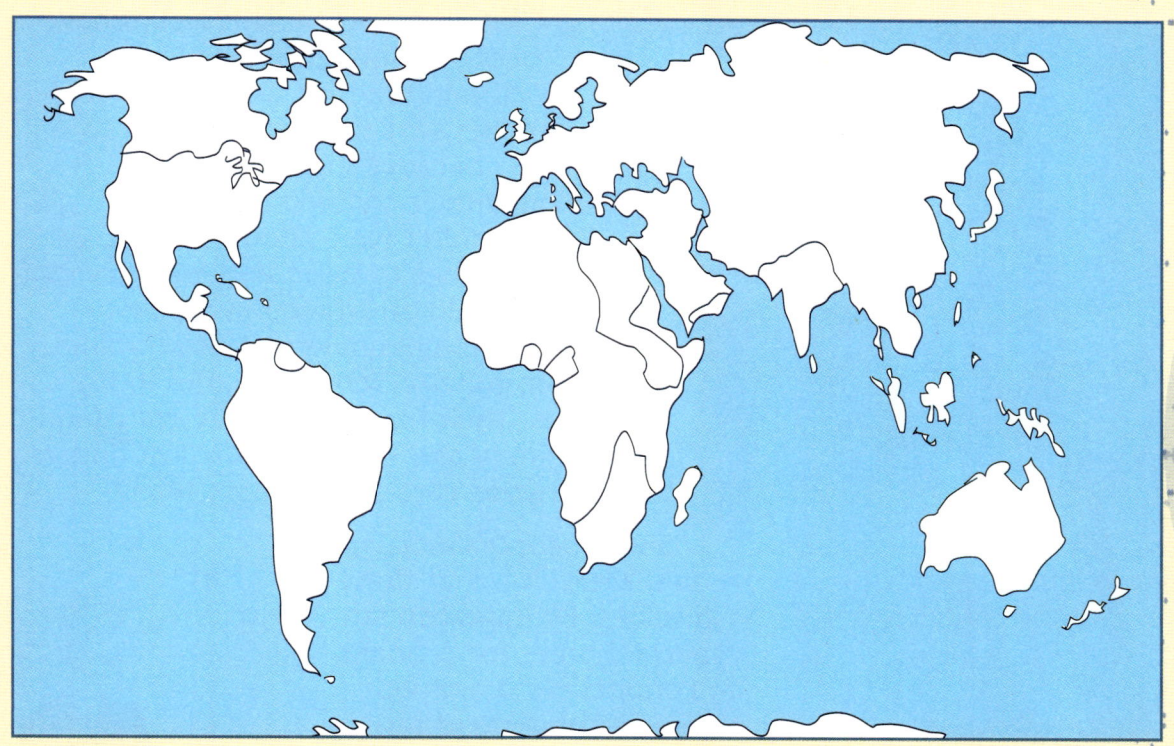

Top Tips!
Find out more about the British Empire and what came afterwards by visiting the Commonwealth Institute in London.

Did you know?
During Queen Victoria's reign, an incredible 230 wars were fought to keep control of the Empire. Many of the people who lived in the countries Britain controlled wanted their independence, but Britain wanted to keep their wealth. Large numbers of soldiers were sent around the world to keep control and many **upper class** people were sent to rule the countries in Victoria's name.

The Good Old Days?

Isabella wanted to find out what it was like to be a child in Victorian times. She went to the Museum of Childhood in London with Max, the butler, to find out more.

"Look at this, Max! It would have been horrible to be poor in Victorian times! It says here that families sent their children out to work, because they needed the money their children could earn. People didn't have enough to eat, or warm clothes to wear, and many lived in **slums**. Children worked in textile factories, up chimneys and down mines. Children suffered terrible injuries in the factories. Their hands and arms got caught in machinery and they regularly lost fingers. Didn't anyone care about them, Max?"

"Some people cared, Izzy," said Max. "Look at these displays. Dr Barnardo ran special homes for orphans in London. He'd opened ninety by the time of his death and the charity he began still helps children today. The Earl of Shaftesbury worked hard to make working conditions better too."

"It says here there were also kind women, Max – Elizabeth Garrett Anderson started a hospital for the poor in London and Octavia Hill worked hard to improve horrible slum areas in London, making the houses she owned available to poorer **tenants** by not charging high rents," Isabella read out loud.

"So there were people who tried to make life better for poor people, Izzy, including the children," smiled Max.

"I'd still rather be alive today!" shuddered Isabella. "Don't know why older people talk about 'the good old days'!"

It's a dog's life.

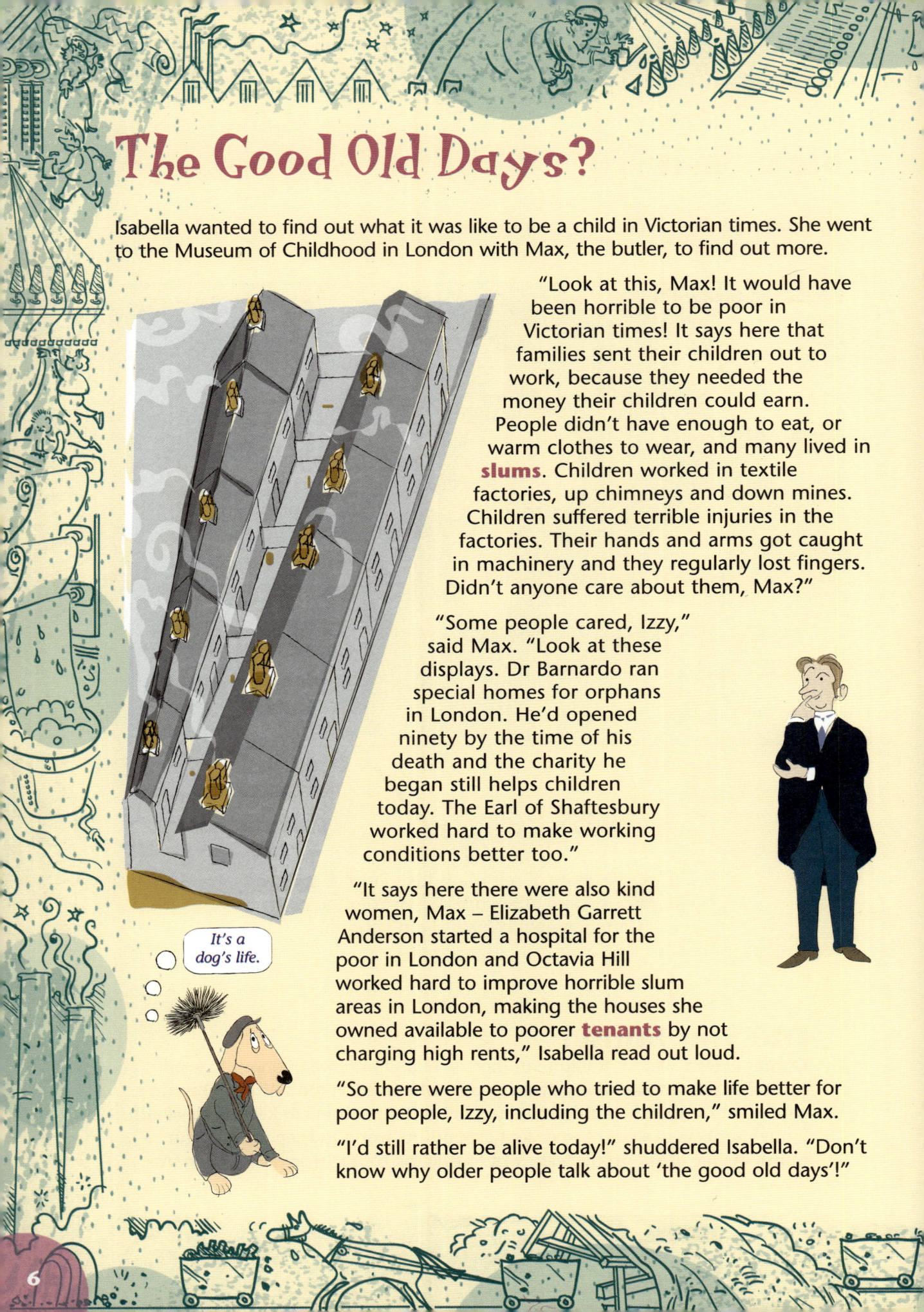

Match them up

Match the person to the picture, to show how they helped poor people.
Then write a sentence to describe what each person did.

1 The Earl of Shaftesbury

_____

_____

a

2 Dr Barnardo

_____

_____

b

RENT BOOK

3 Elizabeth Garrett Anderson

_____

_____

c

ORPHANAGE

4 Octavia Hill

_____

_____

d

HOSPITAL

Top Tips

You can find out more about what the
Dr Barnardos charity does today online at:
http://www.barnardos.org.uk/

Did you know?

'Match girls' made matches in dangerous factories. They were called 'canaries',
because the phosphorus they used made their skin go yellow. Their hair also
fell out. Even worse was 'phossy jaw'. The chemicals poisoned the girls, turning
their faces green and black, and horrible smelling pus came out of their jaws.
The campaigner Annie Besant helped the girls to win safer working conditions.

School Rules!

Isabella came back from school and dumped herself sulkily on the sofa.

"You know, in early Victorian times, Max, children didn't have to go to school. Rich children had **nannies** and a **governess**. Older boys were sent away to **boarding school**. Poorer children didn't often go to school, because it cost money and they had to work. 'Dame' schools taught children from the very young to teenagers, and they were all taught together. 'Ragged' schools taught some **orphans** and very poor children, as well as offering them a home and food. The thing is, no-one had to go to school at all. They told us this at school today. Wish I lived in early Victorian times!"

I'll take school any day!

"That's all true, Izzy. Children didn't have to go to school until 1880. In 1870, an Education Act provided schools for everyone. In 1880, another Act said that all children from five to thirteen had to go to school. In 1891, an Education Act ruled that education should be provided free of charge. Those who did go to school, however, didn't have much fun. Teachers were very strict indeed. They used to hit naughty children with canes! Children did lots of dull work, such as copying out work from the blackboard in silence. Besides, many of those who didn't go to school just had to work anyway," said Max.

"Hmm… and knowing my luck I'd probably have been a 'match girl'! On second thoughts, maybe I'm better off at school!" laughed Isabella.

Word scramble

Some of these words to do with Victorian schools have got mixed up. Can you unscramble them?

1 vcitriano   _____

2 overnegss   _____

3 sannnie   _____

4 braodnig   _____

5 graged   _____

6 mead   _____

7 labbodckra   _____

8 ducteaion   _____

Top Tips!

Children learned to write on slates, by scratching letters on them! Have a go yourself and see how hard it is!

Did you know?

Victorian pupils could be caned for many things. They could be beaten for 'rude conduct', answering back, missing prayers, sulking and being late! Children were also punished by being made to stand on a stool wearing an armband, with DUNCE ('stupid') written on it and a tall pointed hat with a 'D' for dunce on the front.

Revise Time

1 **Fill in the missing words.**

a   The people who lived during the reign of Queen Victoria were called

   the _____.

b   Queen Victoria was a great _____.

c   Her _____ was enormous.

d   The British Empire covered a _____ of the world.

e   The Empire was made up from many countries all over the world, including

   Canada, _____, New Zealand, South Africa and India.

2 **Tick the goods brought to England from countries in the Empire.**

a   Tea ☐   h   Linen ☐

b   Bread ☐   i   Computers ☐

c   Soil ☐   j   Rubber ☐

d   Cocoa beans ☐   k   Precious metals ☐

e   Coca-Cola ☐   l   Tissue ☐

f   Silk ☐   m   Milk ☐

g   Water ☐   n   Cotton ☐

3 **Fill in the missing letters.**

a   V _ _ _ ori _ _   d   Te _ _ _ _ s

b   Dr _ _ _ nardo   e   _ rph _ _ _

c   S _ _ _ tesbury   f   _ _ um _

4 Answer these questions about caring Victorians.

a Who started a hospital for the poor? _____

b Who opened special homes for orphans? _____

c Who worked hard to make working conditions better? _____

d Who charged tenants reasonable rents, so they could move away from the slums?

_____

e Who helped the 'match girls'? _____

5 Match the words to the meanings.

a Cane   School where children lived during term time.

b Strict   Child with no parents.

c Nanny   Stick teachers used to beat children.

d Boarding school   Lady who looked after rich children at home.

e Orphan   A fierce teacher who allowed no fooling
                              around would be this.

6 Explain why poor children did not go to school in the early Victorian period. How did things change for poor children?

_____

_____

_____

_____

_____

_____

_____

Child's Play

Max had bought a Victorian toy as a present for Isabella at the Museum of Childhood shop.

"Thanks, Max – this is great!" cried Isabella as she got the toy out of the bag. "But, um… what is it?"

Sir Ralph came into the room. "This is what they called a whip and top. I used to be quite good at this!" he laughed and demonstrated how it worked.

"What else did Victorian children play with, dad?" asked Isabella.

"Well, Izzy, they didn't have computer games like you! Poor children had few, if any, toys – perhaps just a doll made from rags. Richer children had more exciting toys, such as **lead** soldiers, drums, dolls with **porcelain** heads and cloth bodies, or furry teddies with glass eyes, and arms and legs that moved at the joints. Children also had flicker books and filoscopes, which gave the impression that a picture was moving, like animation. Zoetropes were magical drum-shaped boxes with strips of paper inside. When they were spun, the child looked through a slit and the spinning movement fooled their eyes into seeing the pictures themselves as moving, like in a short film or a cartoon.

"Little girls had elaborate doll's houses with tiny furniture and people, but sadly the girls weren't allowed to play with the toys in case they broke them!" said Sir Ralph.

Whoopee!

"That doesn't sound like much fun, dad! I'd hate to be a Victorian child – even a rich one!" said Isabella.

Circle the items

Draw a circle round the Victorian-style toys. Then draw a different Victorian-style toy.

1

2

3

4

5

6

7

8

Top Tips.

Make a flicker book of a bird flying. Draw the bird on each page, changing its position slightly each time. Flick through the pages to see it 'fly'.

Did you know?

The Bethnal Green Museum of Childhood in London has many examples of Victorian toys, including zoetropes, and is well worth a visit. The zoetrope – or 'The Daedalum' or 'Wheel of the Devil', as it was first called – was a kind of mechanical 'cinema'. It was invented by William Horner in 1834. It was patented in 1867 and renamed the zoetrope, or 'Wheel of Life'.

Call Yourself a Man?

Isabella was looking at a **portrait** of one of her relations on the wall. "Who's this, dad?"

"That's your Great Uncle Sir Duncan Witherbottom, my dear," replied Sir Ralph.

"Uncle? He looks more like a girl with those long blonde ringlets! And look at that little blue sailor suit and smock dress!" laughed Isabella.

"Many little boys looked like little girls in those days, because boys and girls both wore dresses until they were about five years old! Boys weren't 'breeched' – allowed to wear knee breeches, or trousers – until they were about 4–5 years old. The sailor suit was a very popular style in the 1870s, Izzy – especially after Queen Victoria dressed the Prince of Wales and his brothers in them. Some children were even dressed in fancy little outfits called 'Little Lord Fauntleroy' suits with lace collars."

"They don't look like much fun to play in!" snorted Isabella.

Not sure this outfit suits me!

"They weren't. Children wore stiff, laced-up boots – but if they were poor they went barefoot, even in cold weather! Victorian children wore strange, uncomfortable clothes. At the beginning of Victorian times, children just wore smaller versions of the clothes adults wore. In poor families, children just wore '**hand-me-downs**' – clothes worn by the eldest child and then passed on to younger brothers and sisters. They got very ragged as they were passed down!"

"I'd hate to have been the youngest, dad!" said Isabella.

"So would I, Izzy – can you see me in Aunty Maude's cast-offs?" laughed Sir Ralph.

Cross them out

Cross out the clothes Victorian children would not have worn.

1    2    3 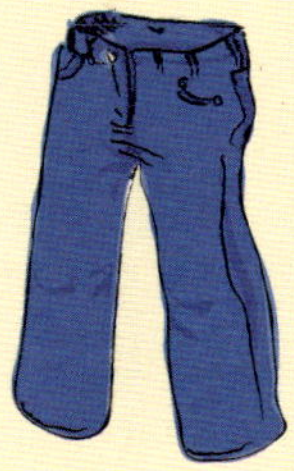 ✗   4 ✗

5 ✗   6 ✗   7   8 ✗

Now describe the main ways in which Victorian children's clothes were different from the clothes children wear today.

_____

_____

_____

Top Tips!

Make a 'ringlet wig' by curling strips of paper round a pencil. Remove the pencil and then glue the curly strips to a band of paper that fits your head. Feel daft?

Did you know?

There were definite rules about how long a girl's skirt should be at different ages. The general rule was, the older the girl, the longer the skirt, so that she was seen as **modest**. A skirt that showed too much leg was thought improper and rude – and would have caused a scandal! We must remember, however, that the Victorians even draped piano legs in fabric to ensure they looked **decent**!

Amazing Ancestry!

Isabella wanted to find out about those of her **ancestors** who lived in Victorian times.

"Let's go to the library and have a look at the **census** entries," said Sir Ralph. "Census forms have been filled out every ten years since 1801 – apart from in 1941, because of World War II. Census data gives historians a precious window on the past."

Isabella asked the librarian to help her to find the files for 1851. She pulled out a pile of dusty brown books. "These are great, dad," she said. "It shows how big families were, where they lived and the work they did. According to these records, around 40% of people at work that year worked in **manufacturing** – making cloth, clothes, metal, foods, glass, pottery and chemicals. The next biggest group were people doing 'service' work – which doesn't just mean servants, it also means doctors, teachers and transport workers, right?"

Where's the sense in it?

"Right. The census also shows the changes that take place over time, Izzy. Look here," said Sir Ralph, lifting a second pile of books down from the shelf. "By 1901, there were more people working in service than there were working in manufacturing. Why do you think that was?"

"Erm… was it anything to do with all the new machines being invented at the time? That would mean that fewer people were needed to make the goods."

"Well done, Izzy! That's right!" said Sir Ralph, smiling proudly. "You're getting to be quite the historian!"

Crossword

Across:

4   Servants, doctors, teachers and transport workers did this type of job
5   When goods are made in a factory
6   People (in your family) you are descended from
7   When something is first thought of, designed and made

Down:

1   Information and figures
2   This is carried out every 10 years
3   A person who studies history
5   Found in factories and used to make things

Top Tips!

Ask at the library or look online to find details of censuses over the years for your area.

Did you know?

Many old **documents**, photos, newspapers and books from the Victorian era are still available and can tell us a great deal about life in those days. Many interesting articles can be found in the local studies section of your local library. **Archives**, collections of documents found in county record offices and museums, can be really useful.

Revise Time

1 **Fill in the missing words.**

a Victorian children played with _____ and tops.

b Poor children had very _____ toys.

c Girls played with dolls with _____ heads.

d Boys played with _____ soldiers.

e _____ books were very popular.

f When a _____ was spun, pictures seemed to move like a film.

2 **Answer these questions about Victorian toys.**

a Describe how a zoetrope worked.

_____

_____

b What toys did children play with in Victorian times that are still played with today?

_____

_____

3 **Cross out the wrong word in each sentence.**

a Victorian children wore comfortable/uncomfortable clothes.

b In the Victorian era, poor children wore smaller/fancier versions of the clothes adults wore.

c Boys were broken/breeched once they were about 4–5 years old.

d Boys and girls both wore dresses/trousers until they were about five.

e Young boys and girls both wore their hair in ringlets/ponytails.

f Victorian clothes were easy/hard to play in.

4 **Describe each of these things.**

a   Sailor suit. _____

_____

b   Little Lord Fauntleroy suit. _____

_____

c   Hand-me-downs. _____

_____

5 **Explain what a census is and how often it is carried out. What sorts of things can a census tell historians?**

_____

_____

_____

_____

6 **Answer these questions about censuses.**

a   What does the word 'ancestor' mean? _____

b   Why was no census carried out in 1941? _____

c   What did the largest group of people do for a living in 1851?

_____

d   What did the largest group of people do for a living in 1901?

_____

e   Why were fewer people needed to work in manufacturing in 1901?

_____

_____

What a Mess!

Sir Ralph is trying to get Isabella out of bed and off to school.

"But, dad, I don't feel well. I think I've got a fever! Maybe I should stay at home today," she moaned.

Sir Ralph felt her forehead, unconvinced. "Fever, indeed. You don't know the meaning of the word. Did you know that 'fevers' killed thousands of people every year in Victorian times? Often the doctors weren't sure exactly what the fever was – **influenza**, **typhus**, **cholera**, **smallpox**, **scarlet fever**, **measles** – so many different illnesses that Victorians used to die from in their thousands. Many of these illnesses have now been wiped out, either by modern medicine or **vaccination** programmes."

"Why were people so unhealthy then, dad?" asked Isabella.

Farewell, cruel world!

"Well, Izzy, **hygiene** had a large part to play. In 1857, 250 tons of raw **sewage** found its way into the River Thames every day – and guess where most people got their drinking water?"

"Yeuk! That's disgusting!" groaned Isabella.

"Yes, and in those days doctors didn't even realise that they needed to **sterilise** instruments or even wash germs off their hands! Scientists such as Louis Pasteur and Joseph Lister, however, made hospitals safer places by introducing **antiseptics** to keep things germ-free. Then, once people proved that cholera was spread in dirty water, new sewers were built and clean drinking water was provided. Soon every town had a 'Medical Officer of Health', who made sure that there were hygienic drains, sewers and a safe drinking water system."

"Wow! Guess I'd better tidy my room if germs are so dangerous – or else get to school before I get really ill!"

Join them up

Identify the statements that correctly state how Victorians took steps to stay healthy once they knew how cholera was spread, by joining them to the antiseptic bottle with a line.

1 Appointing a Medical Officer of Health

2 Drinking untreated river water

3 Building new drains

4 Saving money by mending old drains

5 Building new sewers

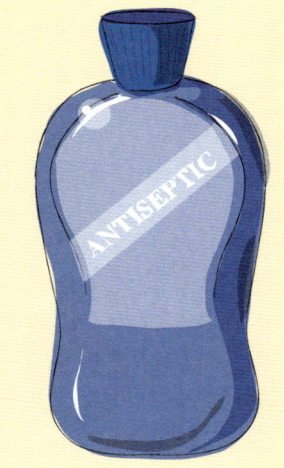

6 Releasing raw sewage into the river

7 Drinking water from clean supplies

8 Doctors using antiseptics

9 Doctors wiping dirty hands on a towel to clean them

Top Tips!

Washing your hands helps to stop the spread of bacteria and viruses – so don't forget!

Did you know?

In 1858 and 1859, people in London were worried about the 'Great Stink'. The Thames had become polluted and smelly. People thought a 'miasma' – a stinky cloud of gas – was spreading disease. Parliament hung disinfectant-soaked cloths over the windows and a law was passed in 18 days to find money to build a huge new sewer system for London.

Left-Over Legacies

Isabella and Sir Ralph went out for a walk together.

"Did you know, Izzy, that both the Town Hall and the library are Victorian buildings?" asked Sir Ralph.

"No – I just knew they were old! Are there any other Victorian 'remains' about town, dad?"

"Well, some of the main railway stations, such as St Pancras in London, and the great museums, such as the Natural History Museum, were built in Victorian times. The same is true of many of the theatres, schools, hospitals, houses and churches that you see around you," said Sir Ralph as he pointed at various stone buildings. "The great iron bridge across the River Thames was built in Victorian times, too. The Victorians were great builders and engineers.

"Look – even this street was built in Victorian times. Its nameplate gives the year the street was built – 1861. It's a great clue to look for! So are the letters on this red postbox," said Sir Ralph.

"How, dad? It says 'VR' in curly writing. What does that mean?" asked Isabella.

"It stands for 'Victoria Regina', and it means that the postbox was made during Queen Victoria's reign. Look at this fancy street lamp, too. It's been adapted to take modern electric lighting, of course, but when it was new, in Victorian times, it would have been a gas lamp. The Victorians have left us a great **legacy**!"

"Yes, dad. They really light up our lives!" laughed Isabella.

The clues are all there...

POST

Circle the item

Draw a circle round all the things in the picture that could be legacies from Victorian times.

Top Tips

Look on postboxes for the different letters – not just VR, but GR and ER too, to show different kings and queens!

Did you know?

Many of our railway lines, stations and **viaducts** are legacies of the Victorian era. There was a huge, fast expansion in building railways after George Stephenson designed one of the first steam locomotives to successfully pull a load. In 1842, Queen Victoria took her first train trip from Windsor to London – and railway mania had begun!

A Grave Situation

Isabella and Sir Ralph have stopped to have a look at a local church.

"St. James's Church was built in Victorian times, Izzy. It's a lovely stone building, full of Victorian carving and stained glass. There are **memorial** tablets built into the wall that remember rich people who once worshipped here.

"The graveyard is even more interesting, though! It may sound like a strange place to go for a history lesson, but the gravestones, tombs and memorials tell us about the lives – and deaths – of the people who lived in our areas in the past. Many of the graves here are Victorian. The **epitaphs** – the words carved onto gravestones – give us valuable historical information. Look at this typical rich man's memorial from Victorian times, Izzy," said Sir Ralph.

Isabella bent forward and read the **inscription** on the marble stone.

"Gosh, dad, this man had three wives – one after the other! Looks like they all died in their 20s or 30s. Why might that be?"

"Sadly, Izzy, lots of women died in childbirth. Look – two of these women had death dates that match the birth dates of their babies. The other lady died of 'the fever', it says – that could have been many things, remember? Lots of children died very young too."

"Well, when they say 'you can't take it with you,' I suppose they're right – but you can leave something pretty amazing to be remembered by!" said Isabella.

As you can see, in 1891…

True or false?

Write true or false next to each statement.

1 Victorian churches have memorial tablets built into the walls to remember people who died. _____

2 Gravestones, tombs and memorials give us clues about the lives of the people who lived in our areas in the past. _____

3 Nothing useful may be learned by reading gravestones. _____

4 'Epitaphs' are the words carved onto gravestones that tell us about the people who died and are buried nearby. _____

5 'Phonographs' are the words carved onto gravestones that tell us about the people who died and are buried nearby. _____

6 Few women died in childbirth in Victorian times. _____

7 Many women died in childbirth in Victorian times. _____

8 Lots of children died very young in Victorian times, or even at birth. _____

Top Tips

Look at a local graveyard and see if you can find any clues about life – and death – in the past in your area.

Did you know?

Many women died in childbirth, especially if they had a doctor to attend them and they were in hospital! This was because doctors would go from one patient to another without realising that they should wash their hands. Infection followed, and women and babies died. Women were safer from infection when they gave birth at home, helped by a local midwife.

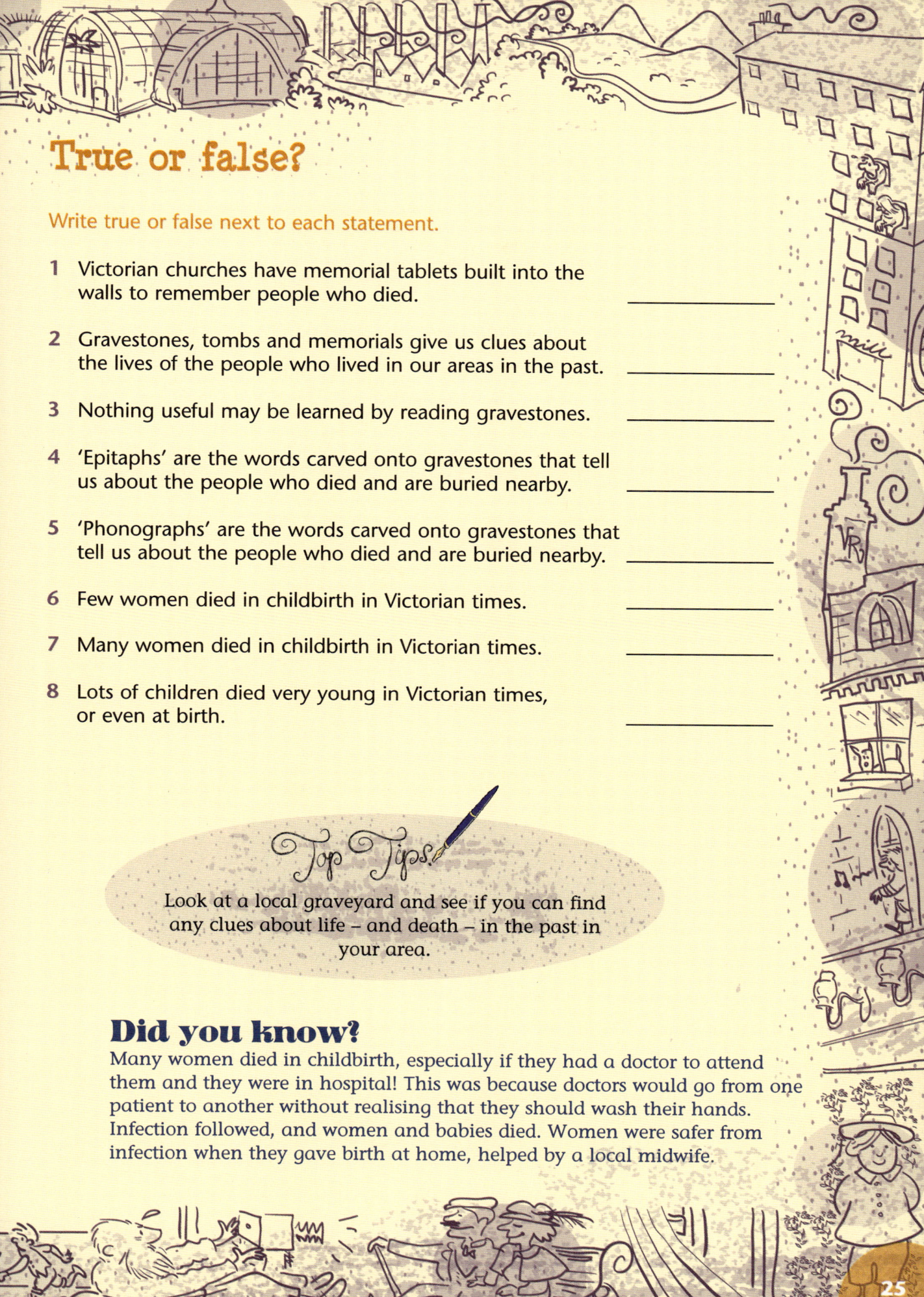

Revise Time

1 Answer these questions about diseases.

a   Name three diseases that were the causes of 'fever' in Victorian times.

_____

b   Why do people in western countries not usually die from these diseases today?

_____

c   Why was the Thames so dirty in Victorian times?

_____

d   Where did people in London get their drinking water from in early Victorian times?

_____

e   How did doctors spread diseases?

_____

f   Which two scientists introduced antiseptics?

_____

_____

2 Once people proved that cholera was spread in dirty water, what steps were taken to solve the problem?

_____

_____

_____

_____

3 Circle the correct word in each sentence.

a   There are many Victorian buildings left as legacies/lunacies.

b   Many great stadiums/stations were built in Victorian times.

c   The Victorians were great engines/engineers.

d   Many new iron roads/bridges were built in the Victorian era.

e   Name places/plates at street corners may have dates to give us clues.

f   Many churches were built/demolished in Victorian times.

4 True or false? Write 'T' for true and 'F' for false in the boxes.

a   VR stands for Victoria Regina. ☐

b   Red postboxes often have the initials of the king or queen on them. ☐

c   Nothing is left behind today from Victorian times. ☐

d   Victorians had electric street lamps on every corner. ☐

e   Many fine Victorian houses are still lived in today. ☐

f   The Victorians left us many legacies. ☐

5 Fill in the missing words.

a   Victorian churches often contain beautiful stained _____.

b   Inside the churches, _____ plaques tell us about people who worshipped at the church, and are remembered there.

c   Memorials, _____ and gravestones tell us about the people buried in the churchyard.

d   _____ give valuable historical information.

e   Many women died in _____.

f   Lots of children _____ too.

6 Explain what an 'epitaph' is and why they can be useful to historians.

_____

_____

_____

_____

_____

_____

You Said It!

Isabella's grandmother was coming for a visit.

"Excellent! Grandma Witherbottom will be able to tell you lots of things about history – from her own point of view!" said Sir Ralph.

"Isn't that a bit rude, dad? Surely grandma's not that old?" laughed Isabella.

"It's not about her being old, Izzy! The things that happen to everyday people during their lives are part of history – and telling us about them helps to preserve grandma's experiences," said Sir Ralph.

"Interviewing family members can give historians a more personalised insight into the past, in a way many **documents** can't. Oral history – actual, living history – gives us extra background to important events and the way they affected the lives of ordinary people. It brings history to life!"

"Do you think grandma would let me interview her?" asked Isabella.

Ah, things were different in my day...

"I'm sure she would. Think about a theme for your questions, such as her time spent at university. It was quite unusual in those days for girls to go to college! Do some **research** by looking at the website of her old university on the Internet so you can ask 'informed' questions. You can borrow my tape recorder, if you like. Your only problem, once she gets started on talking about 'the good old days', will be getting her to stop!" smiled Sir Ralph.

Talking head

Join the helpful tips for carrying out oral history interviews, to the girl's head.

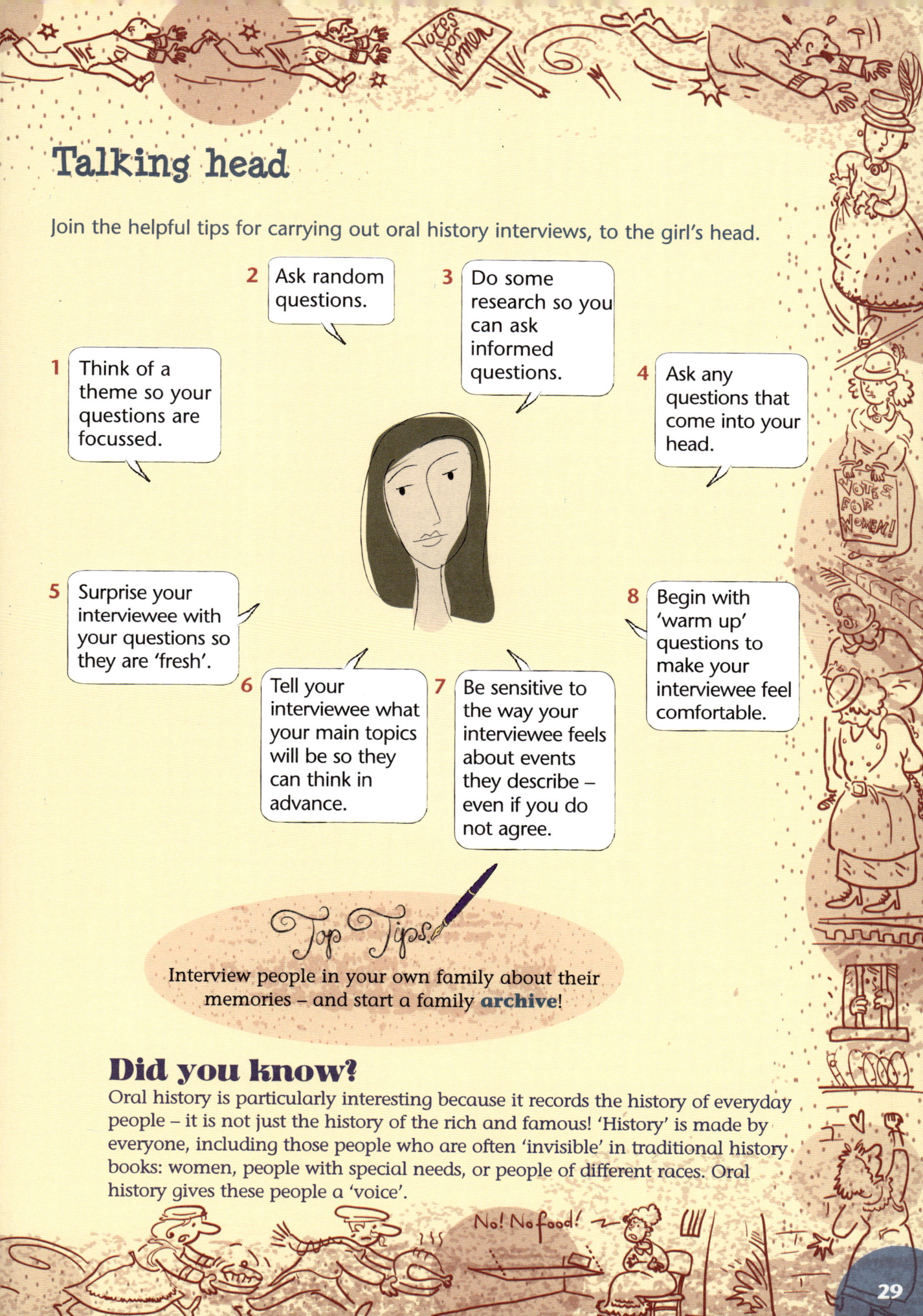

1 Think of a theme so your questions are focussed.

2 Ask random questions.

3 Do some research so you can ask informed questions.

4 Ask any questions that come into your head.

5 Surprise your interviewee with your questions so they are 'fresh'.

6 Tell your interviewee what your main topics will be so they can think in advance.

7 Be sensitive to the way your interviewee feels about events they describe – even if you do not agree.

8 Begin with 'warm up' questions to make your interviewee feel comfortable.

Top Tips!

Interview people in your own family about their memories – and start a family **archive**!

Did you know?

Oral history is particularly interesting because it records the history of everyday people – it is not just the history of the rich and famous! 'History' is made by everyone, including those people who are often 'invisible' in traditional history books: women, people with special needs, or people of different races. Oral history gives these people a 'voice'.

Crazy Kids

Sir Ralph got out a box of family photographs for Isabella to look at. There were photographs of Grandma and Grandad Witherbottom as teenagers in the 1950s.

"Wow, dad! I didn't know grandad was a **teddy boy**! Look at that suit! Grandma's skirt is huge and swirly, too!" laughed Isabella. "It's funny to think of them as teenagers, isn't it?"

"Well, Izzy – up until the 1950s, there weren't any teenagers. Your grandma and grandad were the first generation! Before the 1950s, young people dressed in a similar way to their parents. There were no special fashions like there are today. They even listened to the same music as their parents," said Sir Ralph.

"How awful!" groaned Isabella. "I've heard what you listen to, dad!"

Slick, or what?!

"By the 1950s, people had a better standard of living and there was money to spare. 'Teen' fashions became available and new sorts of music such as 'rock and roll' became popular. Grandma said her mother thought it was all highly scandalous! She used to sneak out to meet your grandad and go to dances in town. Grandad had lots of colourful suits and used to slick his hair back with '**Brylcream**'. They were a fashionable pair, believe it or not!"

"I find it hard enough to believe that you were ever a teenager! Look at these photos of you in flowery shirts and flares – and Aunty Maude's minidress is so short, it looks like a vest!" giggled Isabella.

Put them in order

Draw a line linking two items to each date on the time line, to show when they were fashionable.

1950   1970   2000

Top Tips!

It was only in the 1950s that brightly coloured synthetic materials became available. What are your clothes made from?

Did you know?

In the early 1950s, many girls wore their hair in high ponytails. By the late 1950s and early 1960s, the 'beehive' hairstyle was popular, with hair backcombed and piled up on a girl's head. In the late 1960s, many girls cut their hair short. In the 1970s, long fluffy hair became popular – and today, 'anything goes'!

A Matter of Taste

Sir Ralph took Isabella to a music shop in the high street, so she could listen to some of the 'rock and roll' music her grandma and grandad had enjoyed as teenagers.

"This isn't my type of music, dad, but I can see why grandma thought it was so different!" said Isabella, as she listened to it through the headphones.

"Yes, Izzy – grandma's mum and dad listened to ballad singers, not bands with a great beat like that! Then by the time I was a teenager, music had changed greatly again. Listen to this lot!" said Sir Ralph.

Isabella listened again. "Who's that?" she asked. "Roxy Music, Izzy. I used to spend all the money from my Saturday job on their latest singles. They were plastic (**vinyl**) records – much bigger than the compact discs you buy today! Every Saturday lunchtime I'd be down at Woolworth's, buying the singles and seeing what was in the charts. Then I'd stop by the make-up counter and buy eyeliner! I thought it would make me look like a **glam rocker** – like the lead singer in Roxy Music – but your grandad nearly blew a fuse when he saw me wearing eye make-up! When he was moaning, your grandma showed him a picture of himself in his **teddy boy** clothes and quiff hairdo – and reminded him that his dad had thought he looked weird!"

Well, I think I looked fantastic.

"Well, now you've said that, dad, you can never again make fun of the clothes I wear or the music I listen to!" smirked Isabella.

Word maze

Find these words in the grid.

compact disc

quiff

singles

teenager

headphones

charts

glam

teddy boy

music

s	i	n	g	l	e	s	b	v	w	c	y
h	t	e	e	n	a	g	e	r	a	h	o
b	o	d	n	c	r	l	s	s	d	a	b
q	u	i	f	f	h	a	e	i	x	r	y
m	u	s	i	c	u	m	e	e	t	t	d
m	e	n	a	l	e	o	g	k	w	s	d
c	o	m	p	a	c	t	d	i	s	c	e
h	r	o	t	s	y	n	g	d	r	t	t
h	e	a	d	p	h	o	n	e	s	h	b

Top Tips

Listen to compilation CDs of music from different eras – you may find you like music from the past!

Did you know?

People soon realised that there was money to be made from selling goods to the 'youth market' – teenagers. New magazines, aimed specially at teenagers, were published for the first time, with information about pop stars, fashion and make-up. Films were made with teenagers in mind – often starring their pop idols such as Cliff Richard and Elvis Presley.

Revise Time

1 Answer these questions about oral history.

a What is oral history?

_____

b Why is it valuable?

_____

c How is oral history different to traditional history?

_____

2 Explain how you would prepare to gather oral history for a project.

_____

_____

_____

3 Draw these.

a A person dressed in 1950s clothes.

b A person dressed in 1970s clothes.

c A person dressed in today's clothes.

4 Fill in the missing words.

a Before 'rock and roll', many people listened to _____ singers.

b In the 1950s, many young people enjoyed 'rock and _____' music.

c In the 1970s, many young people bought _____ every week.

d They were _____ than compact discs.

e Glam _____ wore make-up – even the boys!

f Roxy _____ was the name of a glam rock band.

5 Answer these questions about music.

a What were 'the charts'?

_____

_____

b How were 'singles' different to compact discs?

_____

_____

c What did 'glam rockers' wear?

_____

_____

d What music was popular with teenagers in the 1950s?

_____

_____

6 Answer these questions about fashion.

a Write a description of a glam rocker. How did they look different to people today?

_____

b Write a description of a teddy boy. How did they look different to people today?

_____

c What do people wear today? Is there a particular style?

_____

Hard Times

Isabella and Sir Ralph were looking at some old movie posters in a shop window.

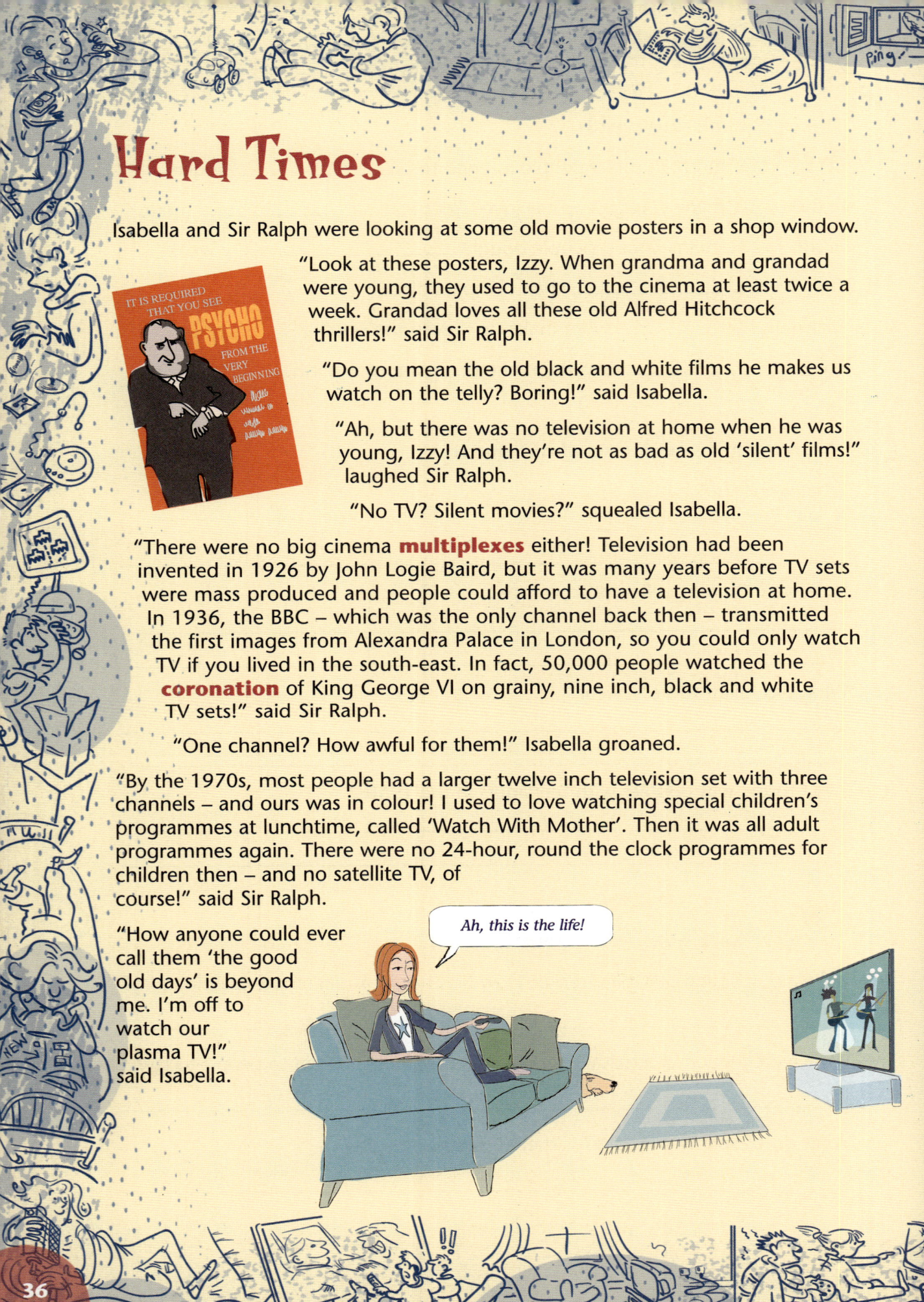

"Look at these posters, Izzy. When grandma and grandad were young, they used to go to the cinema at least twice a week. Grandad loves all these old Alfred Hitchcock thrillers!" said Sir Ralph.

"Do you mean the old black and white films he makes us watch on the telly? Boring!" said Isabella.

"Ah, but there was no television at home when he was young, Izzy! And they're not as bad as old 'silent' films!" laughed Sir Ralph.

"No TV? Silent movies?" squealed Isabella.

"There were no big cinema **multiplexes** either! Television had been invented in 1926 by John Logie Baird, but it was many years before TV sets were mass produced and people could afford to have a television at home. In 1936, the BBC – which was the only channel back then – transmitted the first images from Alexandra Palace in London, so you could only watch TV if you lived in the south-east. In fact, 50,000 people watched the **coronation** of King George VI on grainy, nine inch, black and white TV sets!" said Sir Ralph.

"One channel? How awful for them!" Isabella groaned.

"By the 1970s, most people had a larger twelve inch television set with three channels – and ours was in colour! I used to love watching special children's programmes at lunchtime, called 'Watch With Mother'. Then it was all adult programmes again. There were no 24-hour, round the clock programmes for children then – and no satellite TV, of course!" said Sir Ralph.

"How anyone could ever call them 'the good old days' is beyond me. I'm off to watch our plasma TV!" said Isabella.

Ah, this is the life!

IT IS REQUIRED THAT YOU SEE **PSYCHO** FROM THE VERY BEGINNING

Which came first?

Put the things in each list in order, from the earliest to the most recent.

1 a Black and white films at the cinema
   b Many colour films at a multiplex
   c 'Silent' films   _____

2 a 24-hour children's programmes
   b No children's programmes
   c 'Watch With Mother'   _____

3 a Black and white TV
   b No TV
   c Colour TV   _____

4 a Satellite TV
   b Black and white TV with one channel
   c Colour TV with three channels   _____

5 a 9 inch screens
   b 'Home cinema' plasma screens
   c 12 inch screens   _____

6 a 50,000 people in the south-east watch
      the coronation
   b Most people have TVs
   c TV invented by Logie Baird   _____

Top Tips

Look in your town – many cinemas closed and reopened as bingo halls or even flats. Can you find any old cinemas?

Did you know?

There were different types of cinemas in the 1930s and 1940s – local 'flea pits' and larger, more extravagant 'picture palaces' in towns, with names like 'The Regal' and 'The Alhambra'. These had velvet curtains and could look like palaces or temples. In 1939, an amazing twenty million cinema tickets were sold each week!

Braving Britain

At home, Isabella was looking at books to find out more about how life had changed since the 1950s.

"Dad, it says here that 'after the **Empire Windrush** arrived in 1948, life was hard for the new arrivals'. What was the Empire Windrush and who were the new arrivals?"

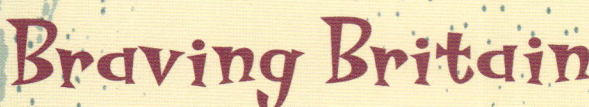

"The Empire Windrush was a big ship that brought people from Jamaica, which was part of the British Empire, to Britain. They were invited to England by advertising campaigns run by businesses, such as London Transport. They advertised in countries that had been part of the British Empire, such as Jamaica, Pakistan and Barbados, asking people to come and do jobs that they were having trouble filling. Unfortunately, many of these jobs were poorly paid and very hard work – that was why they hadn't already been taken," said Sir Ralph.

"Sounds grim, dad!" said Isabella.

"It got worse. The people who came had different colour skin and they met **prejudice**. Many people treated **immigrants** badly. They wouldn't rent rooms to them, and even called them names. Laws were passed in the 1960s and 1970s, making it illegal to **discriminate** against people, because of their race or colour. It was harder to change feelings, though, and life remained very difficult for people of other races."

"How awful! There are children in my class at school whose families come from lots of different countries – and we all get on! They're as British as me!" cried Isabella.

Fares please...

"That's right, Izzy. Thankfully, we now live in a **multicultural** society, but that wasn't always the case! Another example of the bad old days, don't you think?"

"Too right, dad!" said Isabella.

Match them up

Match the speech bubble to the correct person.

1 *We are building a better life in England, but it is hard.*

2 *Come and work for us and have a better life!*

3 *No rooms for coloured people here!*

4 *The kids at school call me names.*

5 *I am travelling on the Empire Windrush to find a job in England.*

a

b

c

d

e

Top Tips

The people who settled in Britain enriched the country with their culture, music, foods and religions. Can you think of examples?

Did you know?

Some people complained that too many immigrants were coming to Britain and taking 'our jobs' – but in fact the immigrants were invited to take jobs that were not being filled by British people. In any case, more people were leaving Britain than were entering. Many people were leaving Britain to settle in countries such as Canada, Australia and New Zealand.

Wonder-Women

Isabella was telling Sir Ralph about what she had learned in her history lesson.

"Dad, at school this week, our teacher told us that, during World War II, women aged between 20 and 30 were **conscripted** to do war work. Employers had nurseries in the workplace so that women could work without worrying about their children. How come then, according to grandma, her mum stayed at home with her full-time when she was a child and grandma stayed at home with you full-time when you were a child? What changed?" asked Isabella.

"Let's go to the community centre – there's a display about 'the Changing Experiences of Women' – and your grandma helped to organise it!" said Sir Ralph.

The exhibition showed how, after the war effort, women were told they were no longer needed at work and were expected to stay at home with their children.

"Look, dad! This photo looks like grandma!" cried Isabella.

"That's because it is, Izzy! It was 1971, and she left me at home with your grandpa to go to London for one of the first big Women's Liberation **protest marches** about women's rights! Your grandma stayed at home with me when I was little, because she wanted to and could afford it – not because she thought that women should," said Sir Ralph, proudly. "Many women had no choice, however. Even today, when most women work, it can be difficult to arrange childcare. I'm just glad I work from home. It means I get to spend more time with you!"

Women's lib certainly gets my vote!

"Which is great, apart from all your fussing!" Isabella groaned.

Design a poster

Look at the **propaganda** poster below, asking women to do war work. Then design a poster asking women to join a demonstration for their rights. Remember, they should be wearing 1970s clothes!

Ask your mother and grandmother about their experiences at work – or at home with children. Are they different?

Did you know?

Today, women work in all the jobs once thought of as 'men's work', but in the past employers thought 'a woman's place was in the home'. It was only in 1970 that the Equal Pay Act was passed, saying that men and women should earn the same wages for the same work. In 1975, the Sex Discrimination Act made it illegal for employers to hire a man instead of a woman just because they preferred to have a male employee.

Revise Time

1 **Fill in the missing letters to spell out words to do with television.**

a T _ l _ v _ s _ o _

b P _ _ g _ _ m _ _ s

c _ ol _ _ r

d _ a _ e _ l _ t _

e S _ _ _ _ _ n

f Ch _ _ n _ _

2 **Cross out the wrong word in each sentence.**

a Today we have plastic/plasma screens.

b In the 1970s, most/few people had TVs.

c The first TVs were black and white/colour.

d In the 1970s, there were special children's programmes at lunchtime, called 'Watch/See With Mother'.

e 50,000 people watched the embalming/coronation of King George VI on grainy, nine inch screen, black and white TV sets.

f Television was invented in 1926 by John Logie Baird/Bear.

3 **Answer these questions about the Empire Windrush.**

a What was the Empire Windrush?

_____

b When did the Empire Windrush come to Britain?

_____

c Who came to Britain on the Empire Windrush?

_____

d Why did they come to Britain?

_____

4 **Fill in the missing words.**

| multicultural | people | paid | illegal | prejudice |

a _____ came from many countries that had been part of the old Empire.

b Many of the jobs people came to Britain to do were low _____ and very hard work.

c Many of the people who came to Britain to work were black, and they met _____.

d Laws were passed in the 1960s and 1970s, making it _____ to discriminate against people because of their race or colour.

e Today, Britain is a _____ society.

5 **Answer these questions about the changing roles of women.**

a Who was conscripted to do war work during World War II?

_____

b How were their children looked after, while they worked?

_____

c What happened to working women after the war?

_____

d What were women expected to do in the 1950s?

_____

6 **Answer these questions about women at work.**

a Explain how the position of women in the workplace has changed since World War II.

_____

_____

b What problems face mothers at work today?

_____

_____

Glossary

ancestors people we are descended from; family members from the past

antiseptic chemical used to kill germs

archives a collection of records, documents, and other materials of historical interest

boarding school a school where children live during term time

Brylcream hair cream used by men in the 1940s and 1950s

cargo the goods carried by a ship

census a record of who lives where, what they do for a living, etc. carried out every ten years by the government

cholera a disease spread by dirty water

conscripted when people were made to join the forces such as the army, navy or air force

coronation when a king or queen is crowned and becomes ruler

decent respectable

discriminate to show preference towards or prejudice against a particular group, race or religion

documents work papers

empire countries ruled by another country. The British Empire in Victorian times covered one fifth of the world

Empire Windrush a ship from the Caribbean that brought many people to Britain to live and work

epitaph a message about a dead person, carved on a stone or memorial such as 'Here lies a charitable woman who led a good life' etc

glam rocker 1970s trend in music and style. The boys as well as the girls dressed in bright sparkly clothes and wore lots of make-up

governess a female teacher for rich Victorian children

hand-me-downs clothes passed down a family

hygiene keeping things clean and germ-free

immigrants people who move from one country to live in another

influenza flu; an illness with fever

inscription carved writing

lead a poisonous metal

legacy something left behind by a past time

manufacturing making things; usually in factories

measles an infectious disease that killed huge numbers of people in Victorian times

memorial something to remember a dead person by

modest shy

multicultural containing many cultures and different people from different places

multiplexes modern cinemas with many screens